Decorating Gourds

Carving, Burning, Painting, and More

Sue Waters

Schiffer Publishing Ltd

4880 Lower Valley Road, Atglen, PA 19310 USA

Dedication

This book is for my Mother, Vivian Kline, because she has always encouraged me to do my own thing.

Designed by John P. Cheek
Type set in Windsor BT/Korinna
ISBN: 0-7643-1312-6
Printed in China

Published by Schiffer Publishing Ltd.
4880 Lower Valley Road
Atglen, PA 19310
Phone: (610) 593-1777; Fax: (610) 593-2002
E-mail: Schifferbk@aol.com
Please visit our web site catalog at
www.schifferbooks.com or write for a free catalog.

We are always looking for authors to write books on new and related subjects. If you have an idea for a book, please contact us at the above address.

This book may be purchased from the publisher.
Please include $3.95 for shipping.

In Europe, Schiffer books are distributed by
Bushwood Books
6 Marksbury Ave.
Kew Gardens
Surrey TW9 4JF England
Phone: 44 (0)20-8392-8585; Fax: 44 (0)20-8392-9876
E-mail: Bushwd@aol.com
Free postage in the UK. Europe: Air mail at cost.
Please try your bookstore first.

Acknowledgments

Special thanks to Kathleen Schuck of Wood 'N Things, in Nampa Idaho for allowing the photography for this book to be done in her store and for encouraging me in all my artistic endeavors.

Thanks to Nibs Glesner, manufacturer of the Nibs Burner, for making sure that I have the proper tips and hand pieces for my burning techniques.

Many thanks to Ram Products for furnishing me with their wonderful rotary tool. It took the work out of carving and let the fun begin.

Extra special thanks to Lynn Stevens for allowing several of her wildlife gourds to be featured in this book. Lynn is a very gifted wildlife artist from Kuna, Idaho.

Contents

Foreword

Utilitarian and instrumental gourds have been around since the beginning of civilization. Since humans love to decorate everything that they get their hands on, decorative gourds have probably been around almost as long. I have seen everything creatively done to a gourd that you can imagine, from exquisite fine art to really fun and funky stuff. Every gourd is unique and wonderful.

This book is written for those who would like to try gourd art. Included are just a few of the many techniques that can be used on gourds. Most of the patterns can be used with all three techniques. By all means, use your imagination and have fun!

General Information

A member of the *Cucurbitacaea* family, gourds are actually a hard shelled, non-edible fruit. Cucumbers, squash, and pumpkins are also members of *Cucurbitacaea* but are edible soft-shelled fruit. The most commonly used gourds for decorating here in the USA that I am aware of are canteen, tobacco box, basketball, bushel basket, dipper, and birdhouse gourds. All of these gourds have smooth shells that make them perfect for burning, carving or painting.

Although I grow gourds for my own use, I am by no means an expert on growing gourds. I just plant them like a cucumber, give them a little chicken manure, a lot of water and hope for the best. I leave them on the ground until after the first hard frost then put them in my little green house to cure over the winter. It usually takes a good six months for most of them to cure. A lot of people cure them over the winter in their garages.

During the curing process, most gourds grow mold on the outside of their shell. This is because they dry from the inside out. If the gourd gets soft and mushy on the outside it is usually because it was not mature when picked, and it should be discarded.

Preparing a Gourd

Since I live in a dry area where I have to water my lawn, the easiest way for me to clean the outside of the gourd is to put it under the water sprinkler on the lawn for an hour or so and then scrub it with a stainless steal scrubbing pad. For really tough spots, I scrape it with a knife. In the winter, I soak the gourd in warm soapy water in the kitchen sink. Both methods work well for me.

When cleaning out the inside of the gourd, I use a kitchen spoon. There are tools made for this but I don't use them. Simply scrape the spoon around the inside of the gourd until all of the inner membrane and seeds are loose then empty them out. You may want to save the seeds for decorating or planting and the pulp for paper making.

A NOTE OF CAUTION: wear a dust mask when cleaning the inside of the gourd. There are often mold spores inside the gourd that can make you ill. I suffered from mild flu-like symptoms for months before I found out about mold spores and started wearing a mask.

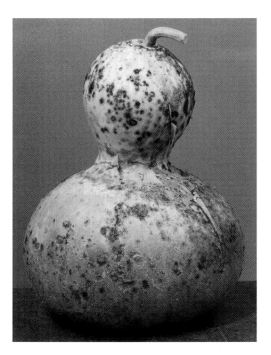

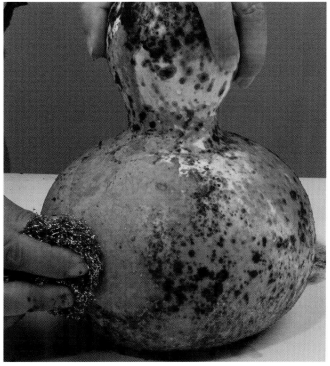

This is a seasoned birdhouse gourd before it is cleaned.

To clean a gourd, put it into a kitchen sink of warm water (you can also add a little soap) and let it soak for half an hour. Another way is to leave it on your lawn in the sun under a sprinkler for an afternoon. Once the gourd has been soaked, scrub off the mold and other debris with an abrasive pad.

Cutting the Top Off

There are several ways to cut the top off of your gourd. A hack saw, a knife, or a rotary tool each work well. For straight-across cuts, I prefer a hacksaw, and for curved or shaped cuts, I use my Ram with a small narrow bit. Make sure that you cut all the way through the shell and membrane of the gourd before trying to take the top off—you don't want to crack the gourd.

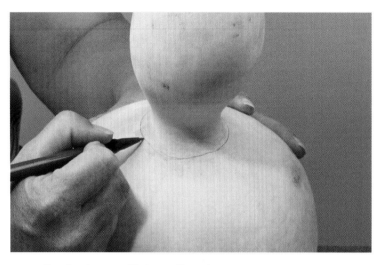

To take the top off, draw a line where you want to cut.

There will be some pulp on the inside that will need to be cleaned out. Use a spoon and scrape away the inner membrane and seeds.

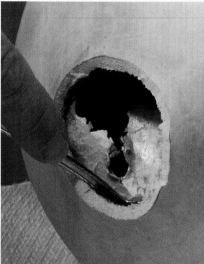

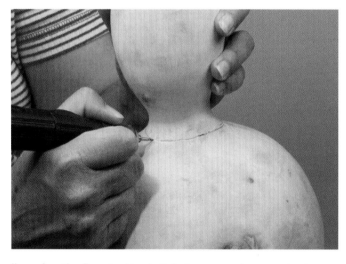

I'm using the Ram tool to do it, but you can also use a hacksaw or bandsaw.

Pull the top off.

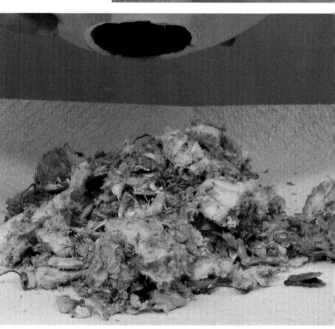

Dump out the debris.

You can pick the seeds out and use them for decoration or for planting next year's crop.

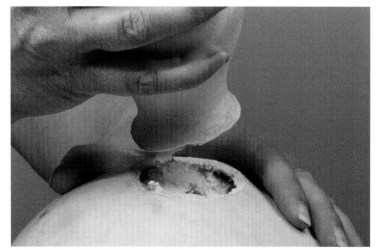

Tools & Supplies

• Woodburning Unit with variable temperature settings with writing, shading and knife tips.

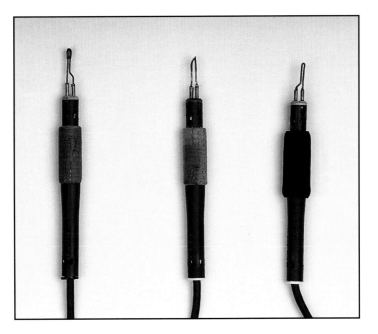

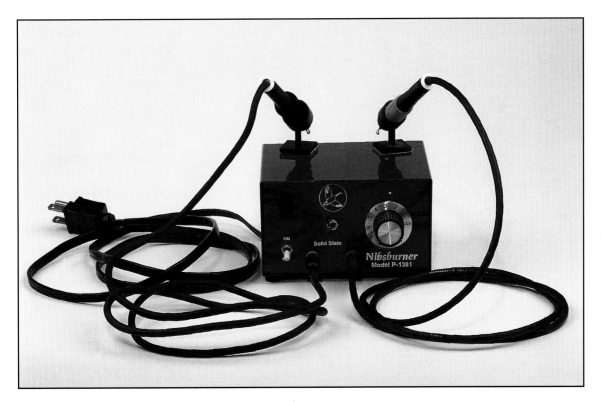

• Rotary carving machine with variable speed control and assorted carving bits.

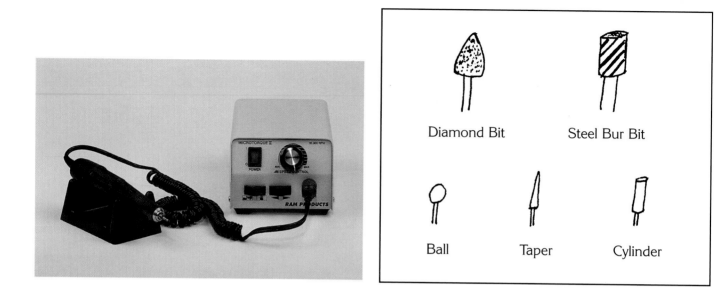

Diamond Bit   Steel Bur Bit

Ball   Taper   Cylinder

• Hot glue gun or tacky glue

• Cured gourds

• Leather dye or stain

• Acrylic paints; red, white, yellow, green and black

• Granite or rock texturing spray (your choice of color) and spray paint for under coat

• Frisket film or low tack adhesive paper

• Scissors or razor knife

• Paintbrushes

• Pencils

• Paper towels

• Dried pine needles, raffia and large eyed needle for pine needle weaving

• Leather

• Assorted beads, jewelry finds and feathers

• Clear spray varnish or shellac

Design Techniques

Regardless of your skill level, anyone can do a lovely design on a gourd. There are two basic tool techniques used in this book, pyrography (or burning), and carving. Surface applications include staining, painting, spray texturing and varnishing. These techniques can be used alone or combined for beautiful results·

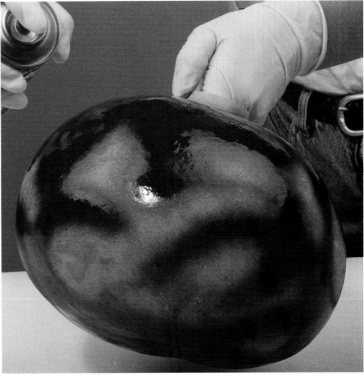

Using a teal green spray paint, I'm spraying a layer that does not fully cover the gourd.

Stone Finish

Start with a gourd that has been cleaned and deseeded, with the top cut off.

Then do a layer of blue. We're aiming for an underwater effect. Leave a little of the original gourd finish showing through. Then set the gourd aside to thoroughly dry.

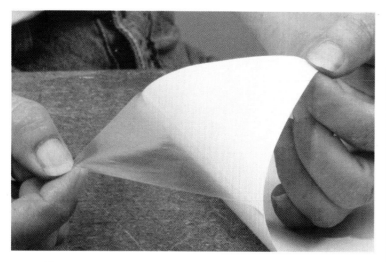

Using the patterns on page 41, we'll make stencils out of Frisket film, a low-tac adheisive vinyl.

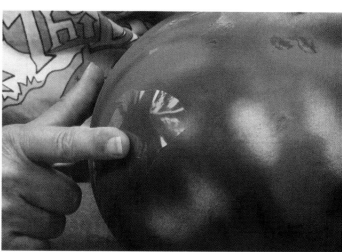

Make sure you press the stencils on firmly. There will be some wrinkles as the stencil adheres to the curve of the gourd.

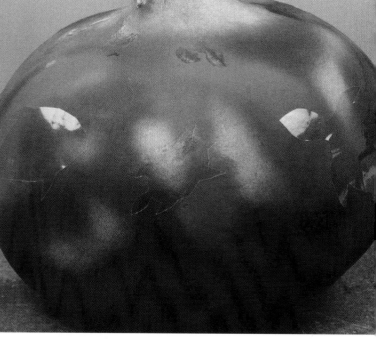

It's transparent enough that you can trace the patterns right out of the book (leaving it on the backing). Remember that with the Frisket paper, the design will be in reverse when you peel it from the backing.

Below: Cut out the designs, peel them off, and stick them to the gourd in an arrangement you like.

Above: The stencils are all stuck on, and the piece is ready for some texture. I will be using a grey stone-textured spray paint, available at any home improvement or hobby store.

Shake the can very well. Spray at an angle in short spurts. Spray lightly enough that the base coat of spray paint shows through.

Set the piece aside to let it dry thoroughly, usually about an hour.

Carefully peel off the Frisket to reveal the designs.

Isn't this a great technique?

The key to gourd decorating is having lots of fun junk on hand to use. I'm starting with a wedge-shaped piece of green suede.

Bunch the long end together and push it into the hole for this draped effect.

Put a line of glue across the top edge...

Glue it in place with a hot glue gun or tacky glue.

...and tuck it into the rim.

I also cut a little strip for the other side.

In the folds of the leather we'll glue some shells.

I used the same stone technique with a bear motif on this gourd. It is a simple process with attractive results.

I'm cutting some pieces of turquoise leather to decorate it.

Then glue them in place.

Dress it up with some beads on a leather strap.

Before gluing them, arrange the pieces the way you like them.

Glue it in place.

This silver lizard makes a nice touch. Be careful when using a hot glue gun on metal, since the metal conducts the heat so quickly.

More embellishments, including buttons and horsehair. The possibilities are endless!

Indian Gourd

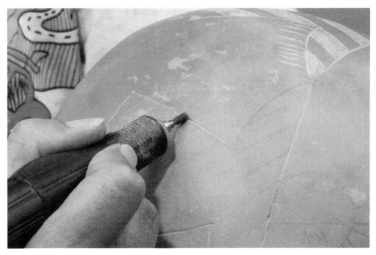

The outline should be fairly heavy. Move slowly and let the machine do the work. You might need to go over lines more than once.

I've used the Indian pattern for this gourd.

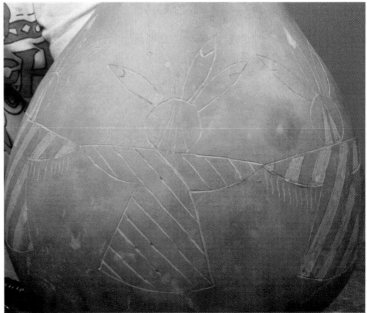

Progress.

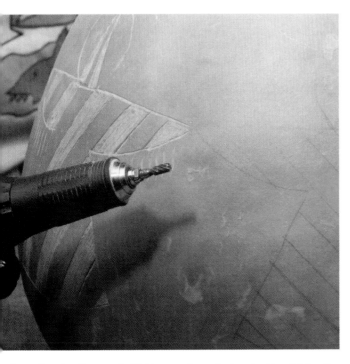

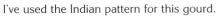

I'm using the Ram tool with the smaller cylinder steel bur bit for the outline work.

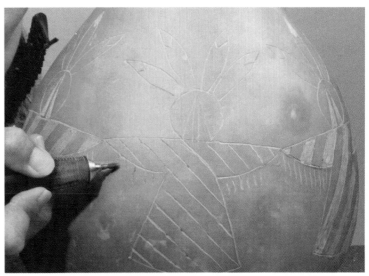

With the same bit, add a fringe to the sleeves.

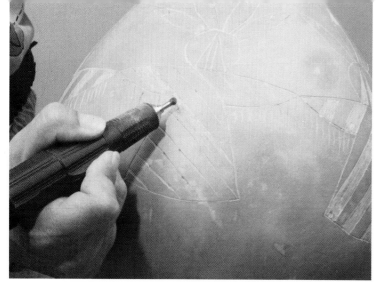

Change to the ball steel bur bit to fill in the stripes. Make a nice, smooth line in one direction. This adds texture.

Notice how the designs and directions of the stripes alternate.

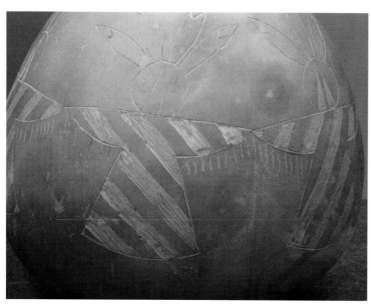

Progress.

I'm staining this one black.

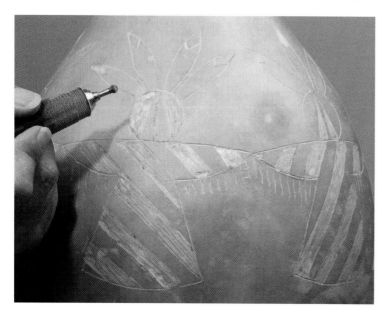

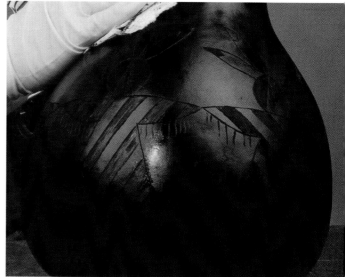

Carve out the face and the feathers.

I've decided to buff the still-damp gourd with a paper towel to cut down on the gloss and let some of the its natural color show through.

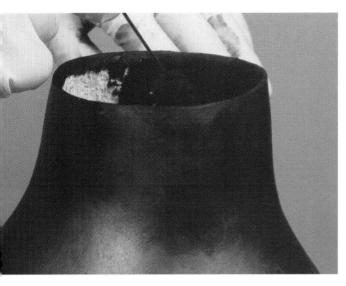

Swab dye into the inside of the gourd as well.

Then tie it in a knot two or three times.

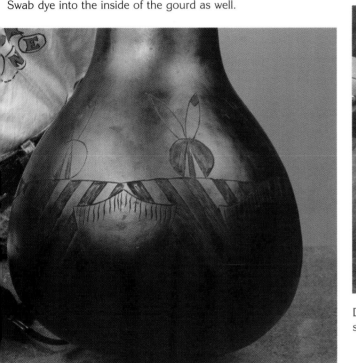

Let it dry thoroughly, about 1-2 hours. Spray on a coat of varnish before decorating it.

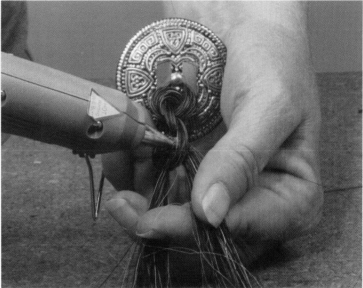

Dot it with glue so the knot stays in place—the horsehair is very stiff and wiry.

Here's a neat decoration. Run a lock of horsehair through a conch.

Right: This salmon colored suede will look great on this large gourd. Glue it in place when you find an arrangement you like.

Glue the conch on over the fabric, and add some feathers if you like.

Carved Fish and Turtle Gourd

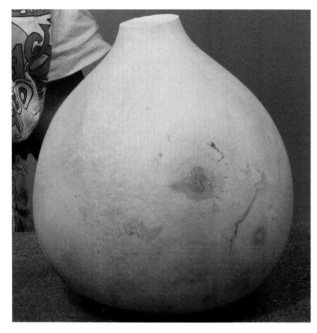

I've chosen this gourd for a carved project.

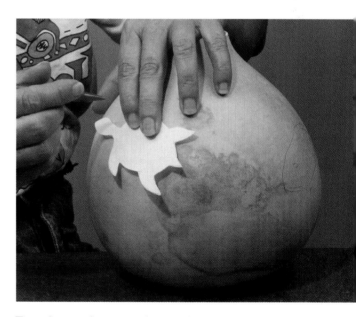

Trace the templates onto the gourd, in any arrangement you like.

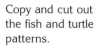

Copy and cut out the fish and turtle patterns.

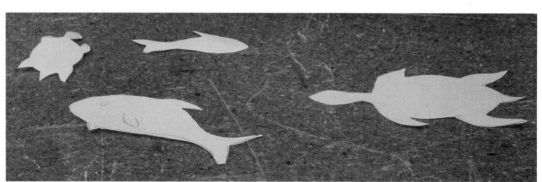

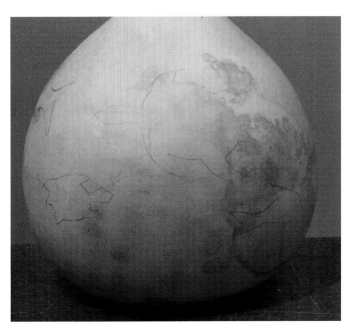

The patterns are traced on.

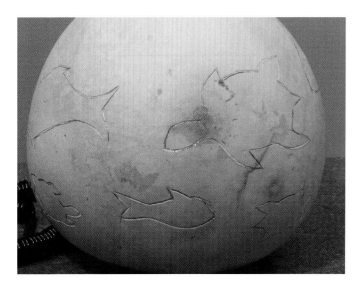

The outlines are finished.

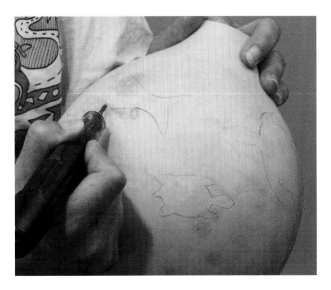

Now we're ready to carve using a rotary tool with a cylinder steel bur bit. I am setting it at a medium speed. Trace along the outline of the shapes you drew, not going too deep. For this kind of work , I strongly recommend ear plugs and a face mask.

Progress.

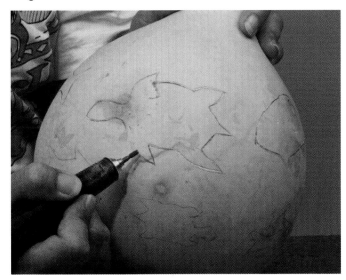

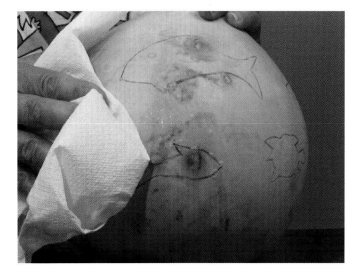

To get rid of the pencil marks, wipe the gourd down with glass cleaner.

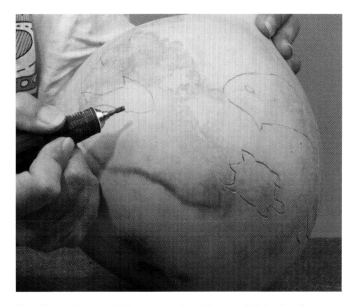

Now I'm going to add basic details to the small fish, like fins and eyes.

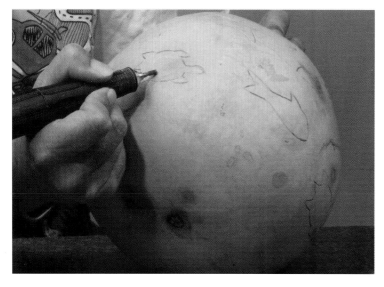

The small turtles need eyes and patterns on their shells.

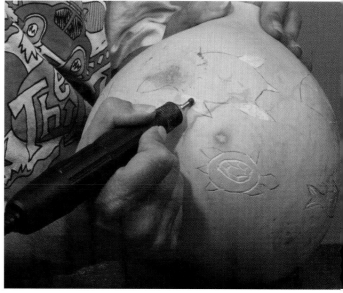

This tip takes away a lot more of the gourd shell. On the turtle, remove material from the head, tail, and legs.

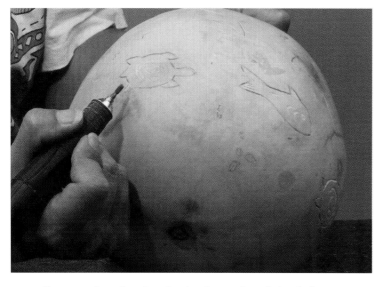

Progress. I am keeping the details rough and simple for a primitive look.

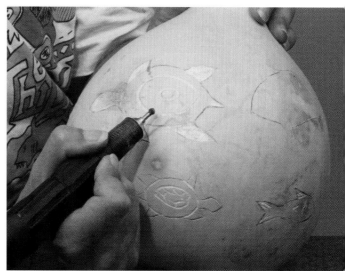

Now I'm etching in the design for the shell. You can draw this in ahead of time if you like. I'm doing a circle inside of a circle...

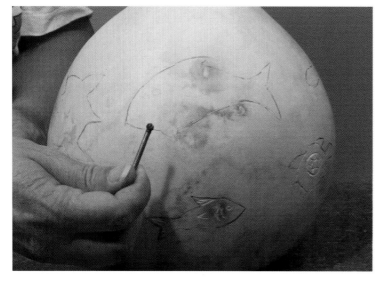

I'm switching to this ball steel bur tip for the large fish and turtles.

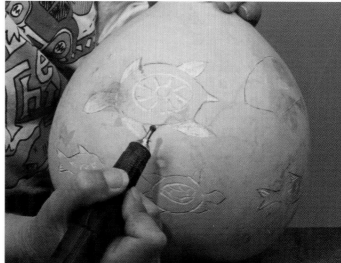

...then I'll draw lines for the scale effect.

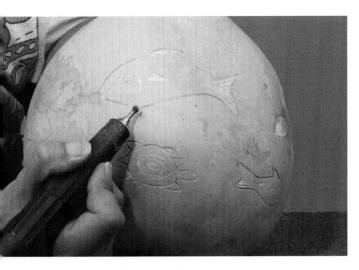

Add texture to the fish tails and fins.

Saturate the swab or brush and then spread the dye around. You can also use more than one color of stain if you like.

Now the carving part is finished, and we can stain the gourd.

It's important to wear gloves for this. I've chosen a Concord shade for this piece. These swabs are great for applying the stain, but you can also use a cottonball or paintbrush. Q-tips are great for tight areas.

The staining is done. Now give the gourd time to dry thoroughly, at least an hour or two. It's a good idea to spray on a coat of varnish as well before decorating.

Loop some raffia around and glue it down with a button for a nice decoration.

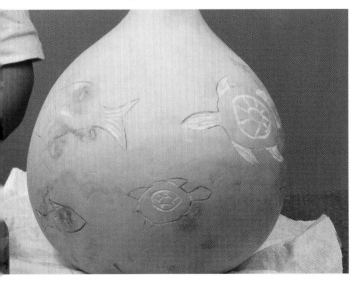

I glued on some other little iridescent beads to add some color.

Flower Gourd with Pine Weaving

I will be burning the design on this piece. I have drawn a flowering vine around the top.

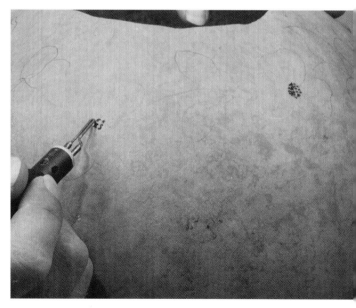

When burning on gourds, use a low temperature with hardly any pressure. The harder you press, the splotchier the burn will be. Let the machine do the work. Using the writing tip, dot in the centers of the flowers.

Burn in the outlines with a smooth, slow stroke. If you need to pick up the tip, reapply it to the gourd surface with a gliding motion over a line you've already burned.

Now I'm going to apply a light paint wash to give it a ceramic look. This is white acrylic paint that has been very watered down so the burn shows through.

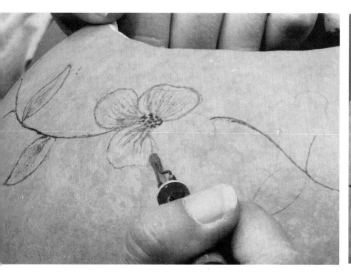

Use the spoon shader to outline the flower and work in some lines from the center of the flower out towards the edge of the petal.

Progress.

The finished burn.

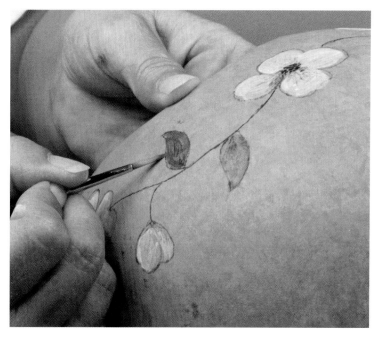

Now for some green on the leaves.

Another simple techinque with beautiful results.

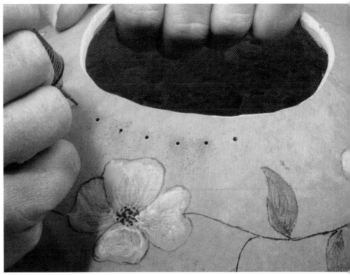

Begin by drilling holes about a half inch from the rim of the gourd. Space them about a half inch apart. Make sure they go all the way through the shell.

For the pine needle weaving, take dried pine needles that are four inches or longer. Put them in a sealed zip-lock bag with a little water and microwave them for a couple of minutes so they become pliable. You can also get the same results by boiling them.

By now the needles and raffia have soaked long enough. Take a piece of raffia and split it, so it's not so wide.

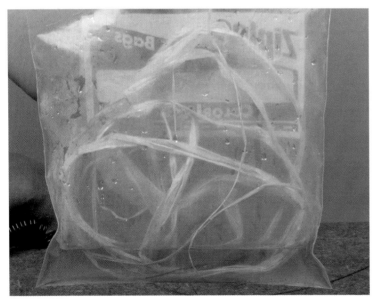

Do the same for some raffia.

Thread it on a large-eyed tapestry needle.

Clip the ends off to separate the pairs of needles.

Lay your bunch of pine needles parallel to the rim and tie it down using the raffia.

Cut a three-inch length from a drinking straw and load a bunch of needles into it. They should be packed in there firmly but not too tight.

Then, using a basic whip stitch, sew the bunch to the rim, sliding the straw out of the way as necessary.

Run the threaded raffia through one of the holes and back out through the underside of the rim. Pull it through far enough that only a three-inch length of the raffia is sticking out of the drill hole.

As you continue to slide the straw out of the way, feed more needles a few at a time into the end of it so you don't run out of needles as you stich along. You will probably be adding more needles about every two stiches.

25

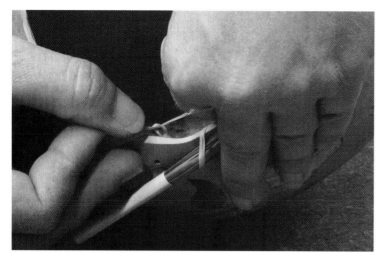

When you run out of raffia, pull the end tight, take the needle off and thread a new piece. Tie the old piece to the new piece with a secure knot that should be flush against the underside of the rim.

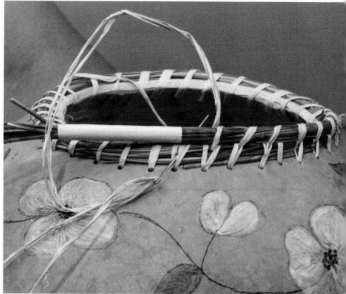

Progress. Continue feeding pine needles into the straw.

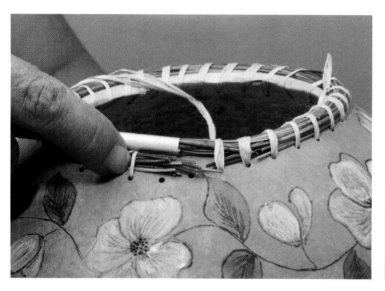

When you come to the end, pull both ends together and stitch the last two or three holes. The bunch with the straw should be on top, so you can begin a new row.

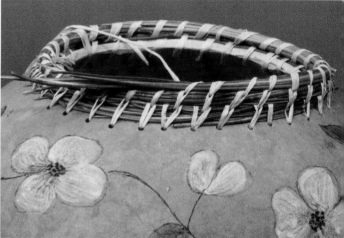

Make as many rows as you like. Once you get to a point that you'd like to finish, stop adding pine needles and pull off the straw. Continue stitching until you reach the end of the needles.

Wrap the bunch over the first stitch you made and make a new stitch. Instead of going through the hole in the gourd, run the needle through the center of the raffia in the first stitch to split it.

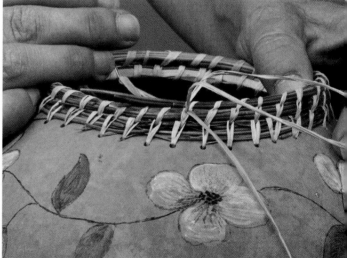

Secure your last stich by stitching over it three or four times and then tying off the raffia. Trim the loose ends.

The finished weaving. As the pine needles dry and shrink, you may have some ends poking out here and there. Go ahead and just trim them off. It's also a nice touch to stain the weaving, but make sure you let the needles thoroughly dry for a couple of days before adding any stain. It's also a good idea to spray a coat of varnish on both the gourd and the weaving.

Gourd Santa

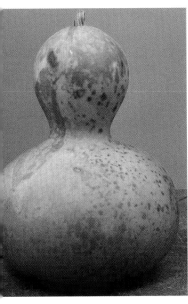

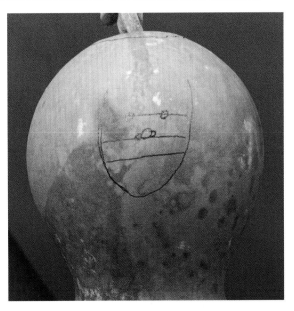

The gourd is cleaned up and ready to go. Looks like a Santa already!

Below: The way I decide where to put the face on the Santa is by looking at the top of the gourd to determine where the hat will fall. Start by making a "U" for the face, and draw three horizontal lines: one for the eyes, nose, and mouth.

Make a circle for each eye, a circle for the nose, and two small circles on either side for the nostrils.

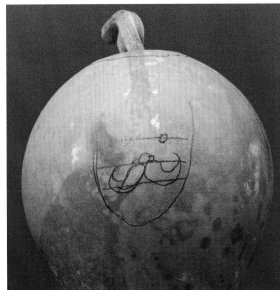

Underneath the nose I make the moustache.

27

Add a lip curve. Then go around the head to make the fur of the cap. Add lines for cheeks and the top of the beard, and a long beard.

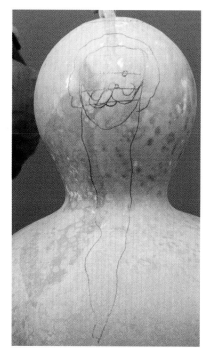

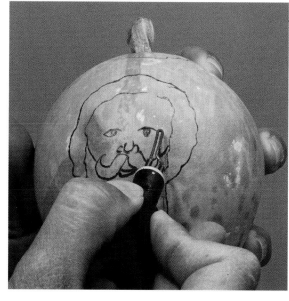

Add the lines around the eyes...

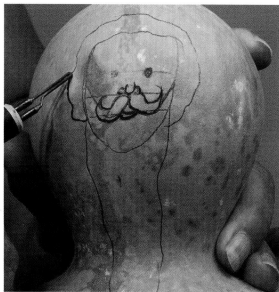

Take the writing tip of the woodburner and outline the face you've just drawn, without the guidelines.

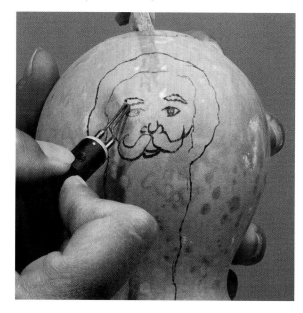

...and the eyebrows.

Fill in the mouth, and add some hair lines for the moustache.

Progress. Get rid of the pencil marks with some window cleaner.

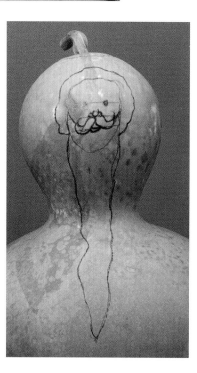

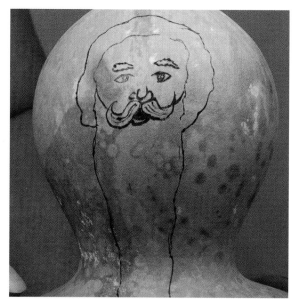

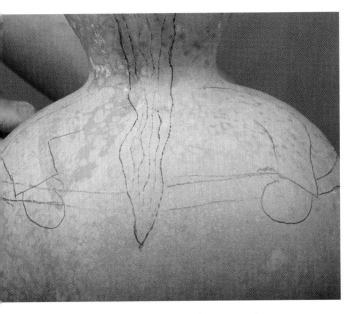

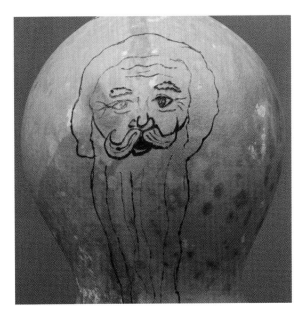

Draw the belt, and then use it as a reference to draw in an arm, as well as mittened hands.

Returning to the face, add some wrinkles and laugh lines to give the Santa more character.

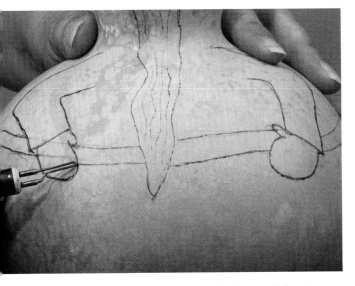

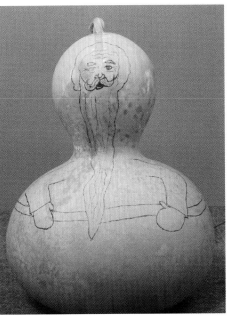

Use the woodburner to outline what you've drawn. Make the lines heavy enough that they will show through a paint wash.

Now we're ready to paint.

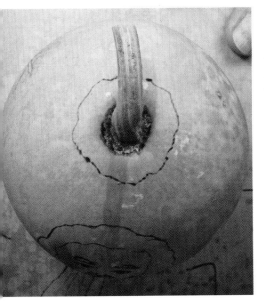

Wipe any excess pencil lines off where you've burned. Then burn in the fur part of the cap.

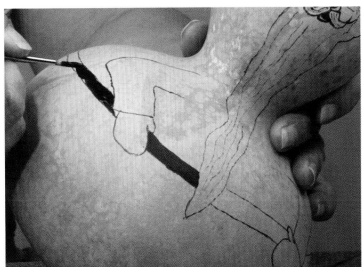

We will be using acrylics. First add a fairly heavy coat of black for the belt.

29

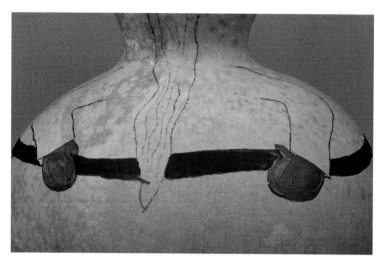

Let's give him some green mittens.

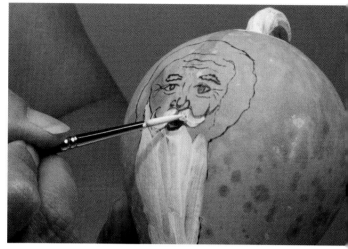

Keep the moustache coat fairly light.

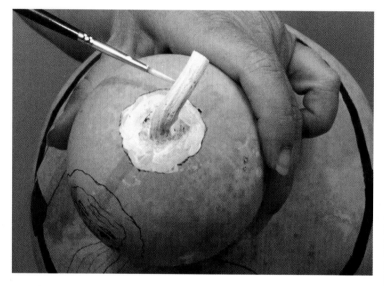

For the white details, I begin with a base coat.

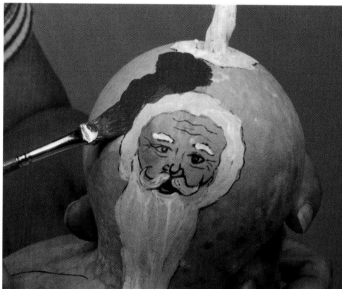

While the first coat of white dries, we'll move on to the red. Thin the paint out with a little water to get more of a wash.

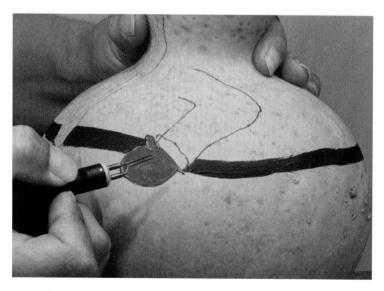

Oops! Forgot the cuffs. Once they're burned in, they should be painted white too.

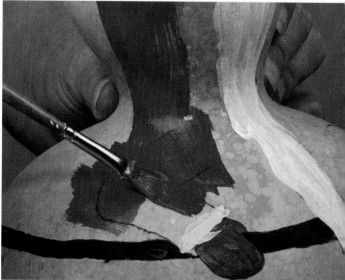

Paint right over the burn lines.

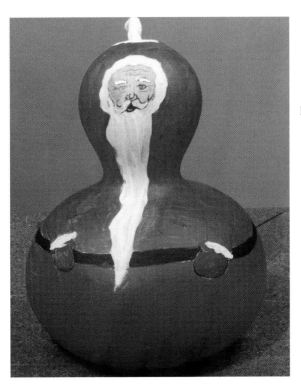

Progress.

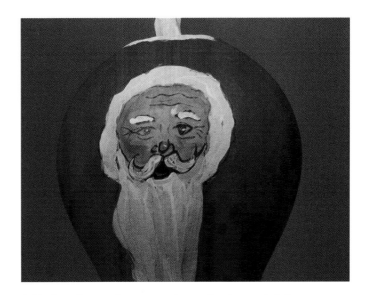

Add white dots to the eyes and nose for the catch lights.

For an ornament, use the top of a gourd and burn the facial features the same way we did on the large gourd.

Above: Load your brush with some very watered-down red, dab it on a paper towel, and smooth it on the lip, nose, cheeks, and around the edges of the face.

Right: There are a lot of possibilities for this Santa design.

Tops and Other Small Projects

Hanging Potpourri

It's a good idea to save the tops of the gourds, because there's so much we can do with them. With this one we'll make a hanging potpourri.

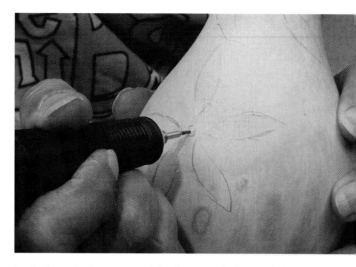

Push through the center of the flower with the tip, following the line around the circle.

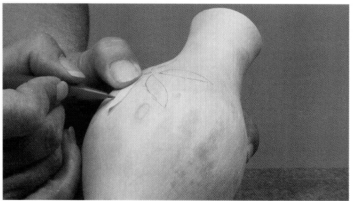

Start by drawing a flower pattern on the lid. I'm using a template for the petals so my designs stay consistent.

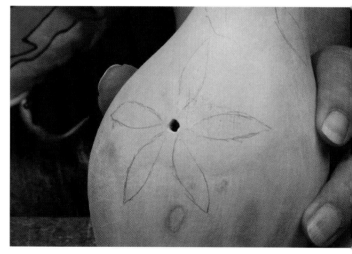

Push the flower center out.

Do the same for the petals. Sometimes there will be some gourd membrane clinging to the inside; we'll clean that out later.

Use a small taper diamond bit for this carving.

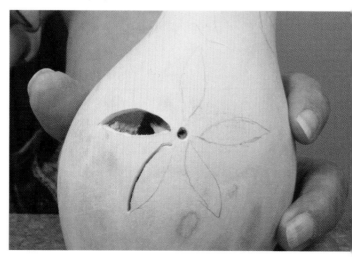

Progress.

Notice there's a little knot at the bottom of this cut that needs to be cleaned up.

Now for the petals on the neck. Use extra care with these because they're positioned on a concave bend in the gourd. Don't use too much pressure—the more material you cut out of the shell the more fragile the piece will be.

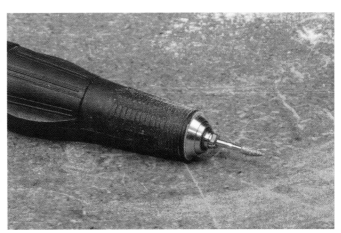

I'm using this large taper diamond bit for the job.

Progress.

Use it to file the knot away and round off the area. While you're at it, smooth any other rough edges you may have on the piece.

We're done with the carving.

Now for some red for a floral effect. Once again, don't overdo it.

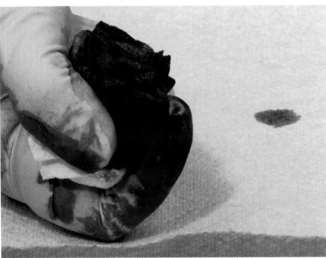

Let's stain it a couple of different colors, and I'll blot it on with a paper towel for a different effect. Crumple the paper towel and dip it in the dye.

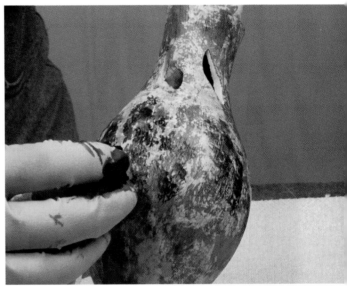

Finally, a touch or so of blue.

Now the staining is finished.

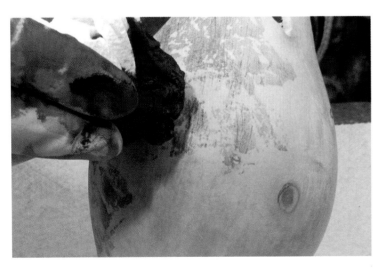

Blot it onto the gourd, but don't overdo it.

A light coat of high gloss shellac gives an excellent impressionistic effect.

Knot it and clip the ends.

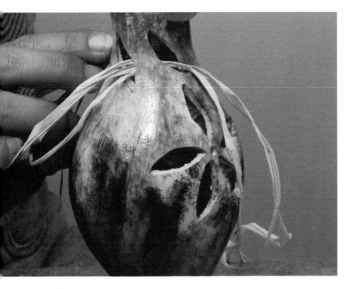

Thread raffia through the slots we cut in the neck.

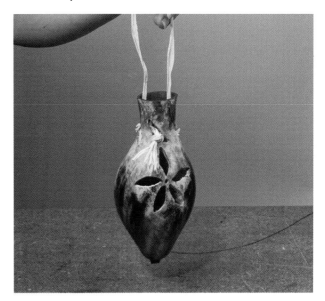

Run a strip of raffia into the gourd and tie it at both ends from the inside to finish the hanging potpurri.

Candle Holder

I have just cut the top of this gourd off, and I would like to smooth the edges where I cut.

I'll use this sanding drum bit.

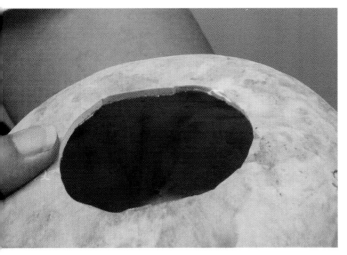

Move steadily along the edge of the rim.

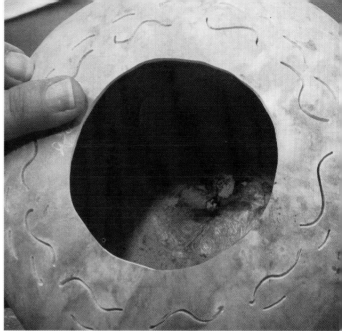

Progress.

The newly smoothed rim.

Now we'll stain it blue. Once you've stained the piece to your liking, spray on a coat of varnish and let it dry thoroughly.

This piece will look great with a small candle burning inside—just make sure the candle is in a votive cup and stays well attended!

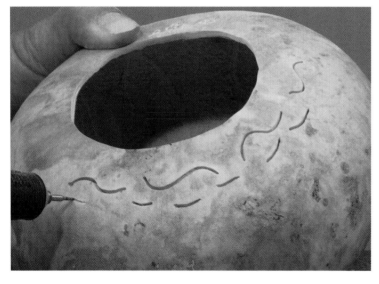

I'm using the small taper diamond bit to freehand a design around the top.

Miniature Lizard Gourd

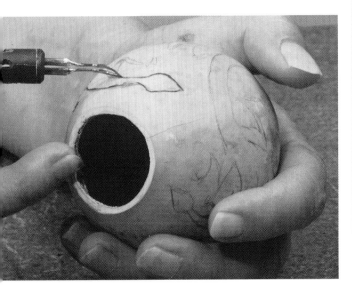

Molly drew some lizards on this gourd top. We're going to burn them in next, using the edge of the wide shader for a deep burn.

The outlines are finished.

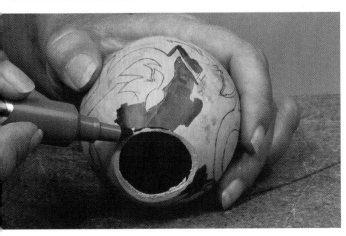

I'm using a blue magic marker for the background of this gourd.

Progress.

Now I'll use a silver paint pen for the lizards, and then spray on a coat of varnish.

Another nice effect using very simple techniques.

Gallery

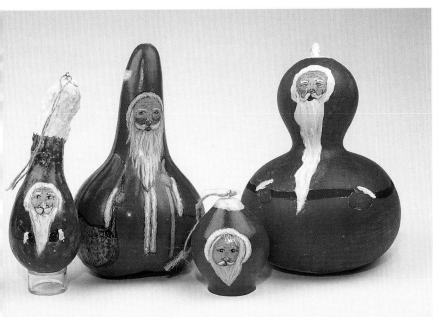

Patterns & Ideas

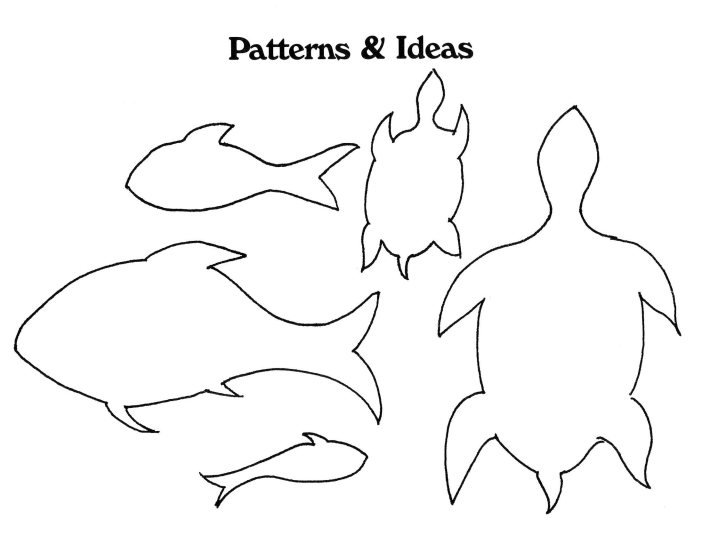

These little turtles and fish were used on the stone textured gourd as well as one of the carved gourds. As with most of the patterns in this book, they can be worked in a variety of techniques. They look very nice burned and painted, or they can be simply outlined and colored in with permanent markers.

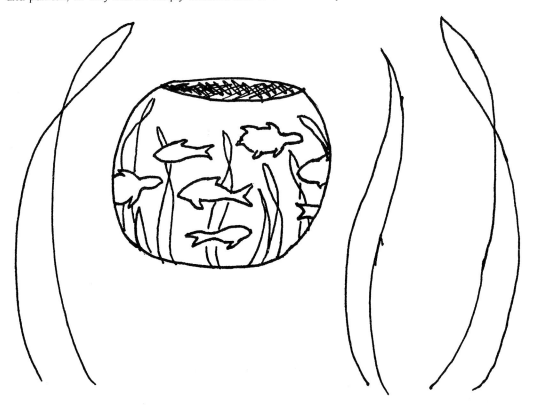

The Indian chiefs pattern is a two-part pattern—the head/body and the feather. Trace the head/body pattern on the gourd. Repeat the tracing around the gourd, with the tips of the arms just touching. If the patterns don't quite fit, you can adjust them by slightly overlapping or extending the arms. After you've established the bodies, trace the feathers around the heads.

The Chiefs pattern can easily be turned into angels by omitting the feathers and adding wings and a halo. For this pattern, carve the head/body and the halo. The wings can be completely carved out, or you can add a feather texture to them. These angels can also be burned on and painted. As with all of these patterns, use your imagination and have fun.

Molly Higgins, the photographer for this book, drew these cute little geckos on a miniature for me between photos. Enlarged for a bigger gourd, they could be carved as well as burned.

This simple flower pattern is not only interesting, but it is also very simple to work.

These are the patterns that I used for the textured bear gourd. I used black spray paint for the undercoat. Follow the same directions for the fish and turtle gourd on page 18. You may also burn the patterns in solid or carve the patterns in for a different look. When burning or carving this pattern, a design above and below the pattern wrapping around the gourd add a nice touch.

Here is the basic drawing pattern for the gourd Santa. Adjust your drawing to fit your gourd.

This tulip design is lovely carved, burned, or just painted. Alternate the flowers and leaves in a pleasing pattern around the gourd.

These small designs are perfect for miniature gourds and gourd tops.

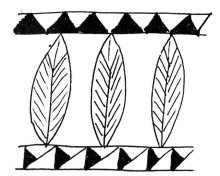